With Your Back To Half the Day

Other books by Donald Morrill

Poetry

At the Bottom of the Sky (1998)
Winner of the *Mid-List* First Series Award

Prose

A Stranger's Neighborhood (1998)

Sounding for Cool (2002)

The Untouched Minutes (2004)
Winner of the *River Teeth* Literary Nonfiction Award

With Your Back to Half the Day

Donald Morrill

Anhinga Press, 2005
Tallahassee, Florida

Cover art: *Improvisation on Cave Painting, 2004* by Donald Morrill
Author photo: Harry Johns
Cover and book design: David G.W. Scott
Typesetting: titles set in Minion Pro small caps and italic; text set in Minion Pro;
cover title set in Birch, author and spine set in Frutiger.

Library of Congress Cataloging-in-Publication Data
With Your Back to Half the Day by Donald Morrill – First Edition
ISBN 0-938078-88-7 Cloth: $20
ISBN 0-938078-86-0 Paper: $12
Library of Congress Cataloging Card Number – 2005904179

This publication is sponsored in part by a grant
from the Florida Department of State,
Division of Cultural Affairs, and the Florida Arts Council.

Anhinga Press Inc. is a nonprofit corporation dedicated wholly
to the publication and appreciation of fine poetry.

For personal orders, catalogs and information write to:
Anhinga Press
P.O. Box 10595
Tallahassee, Florida 32302
Web site: www.anhinga.org
E-mail: info@anhinga.org

Table of Contents

Acknowledgments

I would like to thank the Dana Foundation and the University of Tampa for support that allowed some of these poems to be written. Also, many thanks to Lisa Birnbaum, Rick Campbell, Richard Chess, Audrey Colombe, Robert Dana, Lynne Knight, Martha Serpas, Enid Shomer and Barry Silesky for their encouragement and advice.

Some of the poems in this collection appeared in the following publications:

Another Chicago Magazine: "Obituary," "Ready for you …," "Poem," "Now that leaders tell us …"

Ascent: "A Street," "What would we know better …," "Manifests," "You with your face and I with mine …"

Barrow Street: "A Contribution to the Time Capsule"

Crab Orchard Review: "A Bicycle Called Forever"

DeKalb Literary Arts: "Might"

Expressions Magazine: "Let's talk too much …"

High Plains Literary Review: "To ascend the mountain day …," "That was the year you …," "Tessitura," "Amorous Ode"

The Laurel Review: "Afternoon and Morning"

Like Thunder: Poets Respond to Violence in America: "The man who melts …"

The MacGuffin: "Felt"

Manthology: Poems of the Male Experience: “Each day, as I drive home …” (as “A Muse”)

Organica Quarterly: “Proceed”

Poet Lore: “Syzygy,” “Leather Sonnet,” “I’m supposed to think of loss …”

With Your Back To Half the Day

(Let's talk too much …)

Let's talk too much and wake up tonight and worry
how we get human every day.

Let's argue for the point we were going to make long ago
and forgot in words that change the room's dimensions,
whose shame is ours and imperceptible to others
holding forth, interrupting the unexpected.

Let's scramble the midnight eggs with gossip
and sit in the cinema at 9 a.m.,
whispering that mood where everything could become a poem
(not unlike the money in your pocket
suddenly flying into the river,
becoming the river, becoming
a back stiffening when the sun finally rolls off it
and then bliss ambiguous).

Let's not so much flatter the giants
(who aren't as ordinary as their tells and wiles)
but joke with them like hapless governors, old lovers kept in shape;
they own questions, too, and might
let those disappointments slip.

Yes my broken-windowed friend,
the burrs in Dante's fur need combing out
like the struggle to submit to each voice we might call *mine.*
And there's the old story we wanted told of childhood
that was another frank resistance to the now-shorter life.
On the corner, in that slight at the counter,
and the sense of luck
like a traumatized muscle,
the still beautiful abounds.

Sing how.
Even if boredom seems the way of all flash.
Shall we go down in flaming acquaintanceship?
Shall we balance our blood?
Let's isolate the matter
neither liquid nor solid nor certainly gas.
Let's help ourselves to the problem.

Obituary

— for D.M.

He went out for dimension and returned with the chime of gravel.
He went out to plunge a prayer into history.
He went to clumsy beauty
and returned difficult to say.
Has any grief been shouted out of us?
Have you, too, sought a blessing long remaindered?
He backtracked to the meadow, so tired his sins would not be spooked.
He closed his eyes to approach time before faces.
Wind split him into new sides, clocking.

What's said over a dying and into it?
Has the owl struck the mouse again?
He failed to call back the soul, the bleached broken tortoise shell.
He never matched mysteries. He went out to take place
and was once known ahead and laughed.
He fled the woods with good light left, not greedy but to recall it so.

Maybe you drank next to him.
Maybe you lost your election to him.
Bliss took ten minutes of him. Shortcoming schooled his nostalgia.
And he observed the feast days governed by tender, spitted joints.
He pulled the bee from flesh and kissed across the bed
and returned silent in surrounding.

He goes darkward now, toward where the eyes that don't reopen
cast stars in their stead.
And the night trembles like spilled ink pooling in a handkerchief.
He's unjust in his change, helpless in his resemblance.
Are you, too, sorrow in pursuit?
He went out for a name and returned with crashed raindrops
springing briefly into coronets. He went out to far regret
and serendipity, for the bruised question.
Now he goes inward.

(I'm supposed to think of loss …)

I'm supposed to think of loss when we lie like this
and boy am I, all of it abstract and beautiful
hoping to become a poem which, I now see, can't love me back —
except I don't *feel* loss, and I'm trying to honor feeling
which is not the same as loss though it passes
there on the edge of our attempts
to simply put aside the habits which invest our hands
for our faces not intent on anything but here, its strangeness
at 4 p.m. which is merely now pressing against
our thighs pressed against each other stopping nothing

(Harry, there is no body ...)

Harry, there is no body — only disused keys,
only small things listened to alone. And the stillness of pills.

And there are no blossoms for a morning, only thoughts.
And no rights for a day, only footsteps and air nutty after rain.

Since you're my friend, I don't expect you to agree with this.
I'm not talking business — or mystical whim-wham.

But an understanding. That should get me into trouble.
What *do* we recognize at the end of ourselves?

Summer clouds beyond the warehouse door? Votes from underground?
We replace ourselves most often with assertions and slow spirals.

Distance is a lasting nerve, Harry, and I'm often chased by it.
How far the knife goes in before the heart speaks of whetstones!

Did I tell you I met a designer of search engines? Not yet drunk,
he told me, "Self-reference is an absolute in a relativist set."

I asked, not asking: "So the abyss is just another valley?"
We laughed, and I was as proud of that as my first high-school kiss.

Numbers ... like seeing your shoulder inside your mother's shoulder.
A poem should console, don't you think, however unlikely?

Eager to renew beauty, I've discovered the tall antique vase
and poured from it — surprise! — a mouse skeleton.

So I can guess what brings us to the quayside
once doused with plastic vials and shattered, rotten melons.

The black, glittering slop of the bay night's not deep there,
but we step back a pace from its calm ...

Too much has lain at our feet, Harry, for the mood of petaled ash.
Who's realized the fortune's theirs and dares live astonishment?

That's surely one of the "underreported" moments of life —
yet available as the pine knot resembling the big spot on Jupiter.

Afternoon and Morning

An opened drawer in a rented room opening onto the Pacific.
An empty drawer which follows the orphan full of his seven decades.
The drawer he checks one more time every time before his last departure.
The mother drawer, the father drawer, the drawer of each achievement.
He draws in its odor of cedary deal, the faint must of a vanished Bible.
Death remembers each soul only once and then forgets it
but the drawer remembers, the drawer knows what it holds and won't
confide.
Out the window, the curve of his life begins again where sand and cloud
meet.
No need to sail to the edge of things, the falling-off place is here —
the sudden plummet through an afternoon that aches now to swell
shut …

* * *

The old man must be patient company — no one listens to an old man
shouting.
The old man must not speak his tears — especially those not quite shed.
The old man is helpless — he hears it in the stories he's been told.
Their outcomes — how comforting to foresee them, how foolish to
believe this death.
He rises now more often before dawn — feels it wasn't early enough.
So much of … it? … is ambiguous arrival — blanched afterimage of a
flash.
His journal hidden underneath the chair cushion — no one sits there
comfortably.
Morning is longer than anyone — he readies himself for its scents.
He gathers a bunch of wildflowers — notes: *the hand grasping: eternal
spiral.*

— *for R.P.D.*

(Right hand toward the east ...)

Right hand toward the east, left toward the west:
        our state this wide,
with its shut-in suns and the need to turn them out —
        hours to stretch upon ...

Everything's blowing north — toward tomorrow
        and the day after the day after ...
The woods refresh my soul even as I don't believe in it.
        How to please you?

How to please that horizon beneath the breastbone?
        The meadow's ours
without our choosing; the city: a prayer
        pulled from swirling waters.

Don't we want to be remembered in its thoughts
        even when it has none?
Like the hawk's red tail, the oak leaf swoops and plummets,
        a fragrance broken off from us;

and the lone Morgan horse looks our way
        from its pasture office,
a bridle of calluses across its face. Majesty:
        a miser's grave.

Knock the brooding manor out of your eyes!
        shouts the south wind,
for seasons are uncountable, and life is hail
        leaping from the grass!

What does the south wind know about pleasing you?
        It reminds no one of anyone
refused in themselves. It's attended no fundraisers
        beside the woodpile.

Terror may pitch us into a bottomless stain.
    But the gist endures,
younger than we ever are. Beginning's the text,
    oblivion the tutor.

Might

Fighter planes bank over the packed stadium nearby.
The celebration of distant slaughter,
                                                            the censor's empire,
engorges the radio.

Among the fortunately ignored,
he thinks of poets elsewhere speaking out,
executed —
              their families billed for the bullet.

Hung from his oak, a carved gourd stocked with birdseed
gapes like a yawn,
                                      or shriek,
from the well-suppered life.

In a sand pile, he draws the world
                                                        to be known
in its simultaneous attitudes —
as if this would save us from ourselves.

He wants to add to this circle the broadcasted cheers
leveled by prayer.
                                    He wants the murderous approvers
to wander
            lost in their minefields.

Like the council talking stick of vanished tribes,
the twig in his hand seems passed on already.
He grasps the sand — each word,
                                        each stone thrown
at muzzles of the armored detachment.

Manifests

1.

Those people we want to come back from.
Those we must ignore.
Who could share.
Who would not be ours.

People we dream
and have never met,
and those we wake to.

And those who replace the people
who could not be done without.

Unmasking,
defacing —
indelible people.

And those who return to us
in the mirrors —
unpredictable!

Those who would teach us
or kill us.
Who were not always such friends.

Bored ones we feared.
Cruel ones we loved.

Of sawdust and olives,
placebos and pinwheels.

Those searching our belongings.
Those unretouched.

Who have never been.
Who wait for us …

2.

I skin-colored shell ground into sand
shaped into a castle washed out to sea

I the dish of gems to be set in mosaic

I trademark

Inappropriate experience

Change or die
Die and change

I child in the closet
counting how long it takes to be missed

I blind ballerina
rehearsing steps with fingers on the palm

I the order of importance contingent fired

Five kinds of money in a wallet

Here here each landfall a street

3.

… Cities blackening the fingernail.
A donkey's ear flicking snowflakes.
Buddhas, turnstiles.
The whisper in the mind.

And the hurt which, as it passes,
grows legendary —
so tightly does it focus a time
(as joy might).

Cool vendetta of self-awareness.
Defeat's inevitable homecomings.
The palm's edible heart.

And eternity
rolling down the inside of the ancient's shirt
one rib at a time.

Dawn that won't be kept outside,
the cars on the beach, spreading their wings!
All makes releasing their owners!

The diary and its violation.
Parched, migrant-harvested groves.
Light of unnecessary forgiveness …

4.

You the position of tenderness

You a paging god

You hatcheries
 a carnival of missing fingers

You who travel on the tongue

The vitamin received at the crucial moment
allowing one to think
not at all
differently

Odor of cut grass cheering unseasonably

You romance projected
onto a ripped bed sheet in Bangladesh

You the loneliness just under my skin

You in my mouth can't write an angry poem

You in my mouth make all statistics smile

5.

… Those places we need to drop dead at.
Those places we've never touched.
Old woman sweeping Centerville.
Distant thunder rattling the door.

Locations the crow calls *uh-uh, uh-uh.*
A haven between the eyes.
Children stopping play to watch the stranger pass.
Imagine!
A land where they marry for love!

The assassin bowing,
the explosive strapped to her back.

The hungry archerfish
spitting, bringing down the butterfly
from the twig near the surface.

On the radio, a man summarizing the plot of an opera.

The whole rose bearing its essence
as its lone petals do not …

6.

Us the first war bride off the boat

Us poaching dogma

Us the pearls Caligula served to his horse

Flame tree blowing in late May

Us the owl staring ahead it cannot move its eyes

Us the day a scroll painting unrolling rolling up

Odor of love's nape

Pausing at the rib once to reconsider

Branching shadows on snow

(Lucinda, you know ...)

Lucinda, you know the scattered firewood — grief —
and that rain is rain so briefly, and a scar a second beginning.

You know the hands grasp but the eyes, shy prophets, flee into things.

I hear you: *That want doesn't change, the dead lunge at the living word.*

But what years are these, Cindy, when a leaf can fill the mind?

You know our darkness — one sun devoured by one cloud —
and that no one asks to be born in such a country,
no one asks to take the blossom to ground.

Love's hurting to find its people, you'd say,
          a simmering in the wind of a seeding blond season.

So. Beauty rakes the air, parting day, leaving itself on the surroundings.

In all our friendship, earth's older than air.
We kiss the price, we undertake the rapture —
          a place where a certain thankfulness ends up.

What am I getting at? It's our now, Cindy,
and you repair your silence so right words may enter it.

At least that's my guess, since you haven't answered my notes lately.
          Are you still in life? What have I undone?

I hear you: *The moth is a star suave in its orbit.*

But, in the pasture here, goats clank across a fallen tin roof.
The moment arrives like a hundred dull cousins.

(As the weed weds the sun ...)

As the weed weds the sun, the lab scares its truth;
the mountain hoards the pictures of its innerness
untempted. As the gleaming web grins, the moth
lifts from the split body; the highway lets go; all's incense: *stress.*

When each thing unthings, the right snake is questioning;
When the Möbius strip and the judgment untwin,
able is nimble, singing is stinging,
the infant full of formula where endings begin —

so what's inside of Time, that first silhouette:
The boy possessed of nothing but the beauty of his walk?
The chair and its dreamer still six feet apart?
The avalanche reversed by talk?

As the river-drinking glance meets the moment-weight of self,
drive grace into goodness; see the wound for what it is.
In this motion without journey, make glory a shelf,
the surfaces heavens, the abyss synthesis —

for the black hand, the white hand: pink tongues touching;
for protectors turn to fangs, the nightstick
shoves Godward; for the microscope yawns; for the echoes cling
as the weed weds the rain, as the match charms the wick.

(Now that leaders tell us peace …)

Now that leaders tell us peace must be of war,
        and we dream each night of war;
with Justice under house arrest again
and Doubt a mere redoubt,

I remember that half-skeleton in April
        peeping from the dovecote —
as though the instinct to abandon winter
failed against familiar straw.

I want to blame you, Nature, for our silent tongues
        weighted by the Holy Wafer, the coin;
for old wrongs spawning wrongs
secreted beneath each last reprisal.

Forgive my presumption. I'm just another *kook*
        raging from a public mirror
at the likeness of a righteous grimace,
at the damage carved in peoples.

Our day swirls in its test tube, our publicity
        glistens with art crawling up a twig
to see it, finally, as a twig;
with consolation planning a monument.

And more to suffer now than ever, for awhile —
        and more relief beside the doomed.
Not even joy is stopped.
Who's worthy to accept surrender?

The lies don't cut their own throats,
        whatever some might wish.
And your wild iris doesn't bloom in certainty.
You didn't make us. No, you're not alone.

Syzygy

(for commuter love)

The full moon brims, and the faucet leaks.
We lie in dreams surrounded by books.

Our schedules are "difficult." Yet,
our genitals gleam with "commitment";

the wine's mild fakery evaporates,
a ring in a glass. The alarm waits.

In syzygy, like this lunar conjunction
(a total reflection … or none)

we assume such certainties
are, for us, impossibilities

because *not all one hides can be concealed,*
nor all one wishes bared revealed.

It's a truth now, part of poetry.
Syzygy, syzygy, syzygy:

hear the macro- and microcosm
filling up an unstoppered basin? —

filling up these sleepers with our lives,
the nameless terms and undefined lights

that don't awaken us or school us
in love's common extravaganzas.

These weekends: isn't our play madness
and each parting more adulterous

since it's work we leave for, ourselves
and all that rot? The weeks are hells,

my dear, yet not quite, you would agree —
not like years of syzygies might be.

Who are these two facing the ashtray?
Now side by side, now turning away?

(Ready for you ...)

Ready for you, pencil, to be lost and all the bereavements in you,
all the fogs and home tracts.

Ready for the million mirrors in mica to tease with an intimation,
for the night chopper to circle on the axle of its searchlight conscience.

Ready for you, floor, to gather more flakes from the tree-trunk cutting
board,
its oiled rings of Chinese seasons swirling cracking.

Ready for you, broom, truly ready for you to act like a broom and stop
pretending.

The Lord is chasing me, a cloud in the nail of my ring finger,
the Lord in puppet silence.
The dusk and dawn are perpetual, the pictures on the wall
slightly askew the world is whirling.

Ready now to forgo the foolish correction, the eggs gone cold beneath
an argument please.

Ready for you, banister, to relay the secret of traffic. Ready for you, apple,
to reveal the rush to rust in the bitten place.

A flaw in my eye hungers for flaws in the amazement.
My eye should see out of a rock.

Ready to be forgotten now like the puddle the tiger leaped across in
Tuesday shadows.
Ready to adopt a hundred absences and clothe them.
Ready to drive my friend's road, 104,212 miles on his vehicular existence.

What adventures do you have, pencil, in your new life in other hands?
What spinning storm of cross-grains spawns a pine branch in your drafts?

Ready to begin, truly ready at last to begin and stop enduring.
Into the head silver of the mace gleaned from the silver of old X-ray
negatives.
Down with the coquinas digging farther into the beach sand
when sand above is stripped back.

The Lord of night breezes moves along the battered baseboards,
the Lord too furious for innocence —
ready for me to taste the black wafer of widowhood
and spit at myself who would love this way.

For the nicknames of the elect, I hug the surprise in each man.
By the shaken liquor in the green goddamns,
by the local sanity and the twenty chances with you,
I'm wiped away.

Crystals from the inner dunes collide, rubbing themselves whiter.
The morphine is crushed in butter for the hospice suppository.

Do you believe me? Say nothing.
Hope hunts in the rainshadow.
Hope rappels, licks the world's finger.

In the blows, the skies passing through the voice,
in the moments as pliable as fetus bones, complex as a harem,
I'm used up and ready.

Ready for the street of ugly franchises, saints exhumed and shelved,
biography.
Ready for the dreaming of art works under guard in distant capitols.

The Lord of the bitter leaf, of the pond busy beneath a breeze,
the Lord building roads through virgin woods to the deer —
what is the secret of the Lord's interest?

Does one need again to stand drunk against the moonlight wall?
It's just a life, a meal with wit, departure before dawn.

Embarrassing — a man already in the past, declaring himself lucky!
If he doesn't, who will?

Ready the day, ready the vines and reticulated stones.
Ready the interruption, the shoreline reeds hideous in paintings.
Ready the ready and the variety, the waiting and the unprepared.
Ready the Lord of hopes and canny partitions, and this shameless task.

(Night breeze on our soles ...)

Night breeze on our soles, from the wilder end of the lake:
    our *Don't* won't stay forbidden;

and our voice for friends, the one we can't hear —
    who's touched anyone, there?

Ten million years in a finger of limestone,
    the shirt now open at your throat — you,

my unsaveable! Or is that just me in disguise?
    (Forgive this, if you can.)

Those luscious tears that vanish upon waking —
    it's no good to curse: Alone! Alone!

But we do. Thumb against chilled glass, so near the wine;
    long-stemmed is the next look.

That breeze ... a hike to the dam, all the holding back
    we've never managed, sex

still finding the stranger in us — at least one of us
    fearing it's the last time.

There's a jamb to put the forehead to.
    Our themes endure us!

So the hand goes out in supplication.
    So the hand stays home in its pocket.

Our losses age — so? What's fire attached to?

Proceed

Not to confuse the familiar with the safe,
        the strange with the vital.

Not to beg completion from another's incompleteness,
        nor fit one's self into that wound.

Not to let the days bleed one into another,
        and nothing be noted.

After grief, after work, after the rippling orgasm —
        after the mirror, after the starry woods,

come back to this world, this shattered doorstep,
        this needy world that doesn't need you.

Not to seek revenge and other sentimental ends.

Not to proclaim universals are cloud leashes;
        particulars, unstrung sand.

Not with the paste of godspeech on the tongue.

There is always testimony that life lies elsewhere,
        a child mutilated for more effective begging.

Imagination, like the exile's callused heel,
        shines after distance.

Return to this world, this untumored breast,
        the friend so happy he's unplugged his phone.

Come back to these faces resembling your faces.

Not to load trenches with opposing nostalgias.

Not to see in the live oak another Bodhisattva.

Not to cling to the claw that has already released you,
          nor wear the halo of the first or the last …

(What would we know better ...)

What would we know better if we could lie down in a meadow
with someone we just met on the wooded path? Would we realize
those lips pressing us to ecstasy
were once a rock slide in a canyon, a trumpet,
light pulsing through the void, from one sun to another?
Would we then hold each moment more firmly in our cloud-like hands?
And where do we acquire these questions?

*

And all we've felt or thought is in our words, like silent letters.
We are judged by what we care for:
bright footprints on the Sea of Tranquility;
a villager digging graves with his walking stick ...
Give us this day our implications, and this night.
In a thousand angry, crucial confessions,
we forget that distraction is the foreplay of oblivion.
We try to master those footprints, that stick.

*

There's a bird in the branches that sounds like a door opening.
There's a fallen cypress working its way slowly down the river.
There's a last shaman eating crystals to give himself insight.
There's a Saturday morning hosing a Friday night into the gutter.

There's a leafless winter vine pouring like smoke from a chimney.
A sign under the stairway of the brewery that says *resplendent.*
There's a blond teenaged girl with her dark roots growing back.
The waves in the moonlight spreading out like brushfires ...

*

And leaders pass unchanged through assassins' crosshairs,
and spokesmen claim purifications of river and cloud.
People we once slept with are coming to power!
And though few will admit it, there's a longing for the crowd
which is its own cause.
There are hopes to frame the age in a phrase —
long letters arriving, and the odor of candle just put out.
All while maps change like our children's finger paintings,
while the airdrops continue
and waiters define what constitutes a gift.

*

This man and no other rises, this moment, to his walker in the sunlight.
This old man and no other decides, by standing up, to live on.
Can you answer his question, the one also in your possession?
He picks the hibiscus which asserts his right to further memory.
He pours the feeder full of seeds he's run his hands through —
the dust of seeds, this dust and no other.

And in return for your toil and smile, your opened hand and word,
what did you require?
And what new agreement, wholly your own, mixes on your tongue now
with the aftertaste of self-pity?
Good-bye, life of defensible postponements!
Good-byc, lifc of customary triumphs!
We should have dined more often, should have slept together.
We're the scarf around the throat revealing age.

We're the thankyou cake, the farewells sliced into equal portions.
How could I forget you, piece by piece?

*

So one bright winter afternoon they gather and hover over you,
some of those you wounded and betrayed, chasing your mirage.
They bother to congregate not so much to haunt you
as to remind how little of your nature you don't countenance.
It's no revenge, this instruction in your ignorance, but a gift to your
dead self
from all that can't be changed.

*

There's always a man offering a fake fossil or token,
in a hushed voice as though only you appreciate
the rare, the ancient, the magical.
Whatever his illusion, he's offering you the cure —
your malady: wanting to know the world.
You look away, of course, and say *No, thank you*,
relieved that you won't bargain with yourself.
You have ruins to visit, a famous tomb,
and step away and, like a morning drunk, turn your ankle on the
cobbles.
But you see the ghosts there, along the Prado, the leaves blowing.
You're not going anywhere he can't find you —
who all look alike to him,
who may then be ready to stop and listen.

*

We have our street to shout down, our avenue in a hurry
to ignore the truths of ragged tongues. Streets of this sort daydream.
Their tree trunks gape where branches have been lopped off.
In the wet night, a stray palm frond may brush a high tension wire and
spark …
And some cradle a book in their laps, trying to bring the world closer.
Comfort me, a lover says, hoping to help,
knowing the beloved is prone to suggestion.
Why would we think this tale different from our own?
A man possessed experience without knowledge —
the suit in the closet, a stub in the pocket.
He stood before his house, at the moon-splashed curb,
frightened by his laughter at himself.

*

No perfect moment, no moments to perfect.
Who will ask the questions over wine and open to us
the voice that might surprise us with our truth?
We sit together amid talk and no talk
who live by what we have forgotten, trying to awaken.
Time: golden crumbs and the last grape on a white platter.
What taste lies in you now housed in a pressed blazer?
You with the devouring laugh, my friend, you are my friend —
the meals under these red awnings declare it.
Who are you before the mirror, in a field alone, on your knees?

A Street

Here is an old woman, blind Daisy,
        and the girls who tease her.
Here is a rotting birdhouse.
Here is the porch where Greg first kissed Tangie,
        who moved away,
        and here are sand burrs.
Croquet in the Standleys' yard at evening,
        and I sit on the wall, aged ten, and watch.
Here is the invitation, at last, to join the adults,
        and a red glove budding from a snow fort in spring.
Here is a culvert where Lenny and I hid
        from dinosaurs,
Lenny dead from cardiac arrest at eighteen.
Here is a mouse grave under the apricot tree.
Here is where Dad drank iced tea
        after working on the new addition.
Mom's cigarette glows so lonely in the breezeway.
Here are the black beetles with pincers,
        and the smell of rusted screens pressed against my cheek.
Here is a dog snoring on its chain.
Here is the first erection and first jism
        glittering on kindling behind the garage.
Our secret club let Mick join because of it.
Here we are, sleeping out,
        our flashlights pushing back the uppermost leaves.
Wrestlers flip each other on TV.
Cheeseburgers at midnight.
Here are mornings like a rake with its teeth clamping the dirt.
Here is the nearly-finished ranch house at the bottom of the hill,
        black plastic over its windows,
        until it's torn down.
Here are the globe coffee cups and the salt shaker collection
        longing for the ocean,
and the monkey drummer in the bottom of Mom's closet,

Mom's money tucked into its feet,
where the batteries should go.
"All gone," says Dave's kid sister Patty,
holding up her bowl.
Here are the baskets I shoot in the driveway all winter —
two hundred a day to make the team —
and the baskets I shoot with Dale,
four years older than I but younger, mentally,
who can't make any team.
He wants to be a cartoonist.
I want to kiss Lena.
All gone.
Not from wars or famine.
Not from the green, June sky
swinging a fist of wind
from its sultry silence.
Gone, in my middle age,
like the Christmas pines burned in our clubhouse stove.
Here are the hooks for a porch swing,
hooks for holding up the stars.
Here is Mr. Downing's head in a cardboard box
so he can look at the eclipse.
Toy trains ran through that pink split-level.
Who will tell its new owners?
Here is Tom's solarium, a scorpion encased in plastic
holding down papers,
his finger stirring his dad's ashes
in a beer stein from the mantel.
Here is Grandma's smile
in a bathroom jar,
and an afternoon of fat, baker's-dozen minutes.
Here are clouds and the way I look at them
when things should mean more,
when I am proud to belong
among these people.

Here are my street's turnings
            into other streets, other bloodlines
            you never come back to
            no matter
            how round the world.
Through my bedroom window floats the odor of lilac
            and mosquito repellant.
            Mom laughs. Uncle Lou slaps his legs
            and wants everyone to listen,
            a cigarette wagging in his mouth.
My brother grumbles and rolls over in the darkness.
We were still dressed alike, then.
I am too much a spectator.
No one should want a time back.
Here is the hopeful inattention of families to themselves.
Here is the convertible
            Mick pretended to be on my bike.
Here is the small lie we caught Dad in,
            and our smiles to ourselves,
            and the outs I caught at first base.
Here is Lenny's mom calling him home to supper,
            calling the evening by his name.

(We master nothing …)

We master nothing, James. So much for confession.
Douse a fire too quickly and ash dusts the hand.

Old friends such as we, are one ringing horizon
spun from children brought together once by a ball.

The soft, ragged shirt of a voice; the glass bearing an idea:
prints of last night's rain in the sandy path.

We might ask, though it's not our knee to go down on,
what weight objects take as they foul or sing.

Our own age — how can it be
when others walk through us, arriving with our gestures?

Death's lifted the chin of those we've loved ill.
Until a hand grabs it, a cloud knows no agony.

I'm ashamed to be chasing through this morning
one thing I've done not a failure.

That dandelion, blond with late seed,
is shaking apart on the slightest breeze across us.

(Each day, as I drive home ...)

Each day, as I drive home, I pass the boy selling his body on the corner.

Each day he offers a different body,
but he gazes at me with the same frankness
I would call accusing — since it seems he knows something true about
me.

After all, he deals with those most interested in themselves, helpless
to be otherwise, even if they ask a few questions of others in
conversation,

or enumerate in poems the perversities available
to one who would describe things.

He disturbs me because — as my eye grazes the white shirt
draped over his bared shoulder,

as it flutters and flees his suspiciously compact waist —
I feel one of us must apologize.

My secret lust does not include him, but he gives it a face with his need.
And he surmises, no doubt, its customary wishes

from the furtive cat-calls of others passing,
in the savagery of the tender-hearted
who stop and lean toward him from behind half-lowered windows,

offering help. I don't wish

to confuse soul with money here, though
the one symbol is exchanged regularly for the other,
verifying why people meet sometimes as they do.

His gaze pursues, asking: *Are you sure?*
And I'm not.

Because how often now I fall behind the life reputed to be mine,
                                                                                dedicated
to it because I've made enough of it

I would like to make it more —
though who comprehends that work, that luxury and luck, ever?

And he, who nibbles glassy, salted junk from the gas station deli,
and hums to himself a top-forty lyric, keeping it close
like a bodyguard accompanying him into the darkest vehicles,

he's going to live forever.

And it has nothing to do with the bougainvillea bursting here and there
from these drought months, their green leaves
suddenly a rife blush against the strain.

It has nothing to do with that transformation, or any which we miss,
impatient for something else.

Felt

Covetous of facile combinations,
of the cue ball's neutrality
in displaying, shot after shot,
intention and ability,
the men and women at the tables
know this game of surfaces,
momentum and control —

if knowledge rests in learning how to play
the poor lie and the easy leave,
the comely angle and the scratch,
with all the equanimity
one brings to those peopled encounters
from the inexhaustible
pool of situations.

In other words: No Way. One gets snookered;
one double kisses, or misstrokes —
or hits upon undiscovered
english which even the experts,
to their amazement, can't replicate:
touch, more than fine equipment,
defying all physics.

Cushioned by a round of drinks and side bets,
this arena of the passions
accommodates the friendly rack
and makes room for exhibitions;
though a match may end in sudden death,
the game itself continues;
each gets a turn, sometimes.

Underlying all, the ancient fabric —
    which the ancients thought barbaric
    (though there are coarser wraps for sense) —
        stretches its synthetic limits
    like an ultimate shade, a given
      worn thin and new. Beneath that
         is spotless, leveled slate.

Leather Sonnet

Already old fashioned, this style of edge,
this black-strapped kinkiness, this hellion crop:
a shriveling peach in the tattooed biceps;
a rotting rose in the pasty a badge.

Bondage and bonding, perving for purview —
it purrs as the moves are put on, the tack:
the club night meeting actuarial tact
like a sofa under a laser show.

So, chaps in hiding hiding chaps; the call
of the wild: submit, dominate tricks …
or something drunker, hornier, that sticks
in the glassy pinkness of the be-all.

Put it on, says the mind, to take it off.
Take it on, says the heart, to put it off.

(Lovelier than most ambition …)

Lovelier than most ambition: the grit between floor planks.
More eloquent than most complaint: the tabby's claw
put lightly to its master's temple,
the master easing down that character.

Who tore themselves apart as they sank into flowers
tried to love us, too. The stink of heartwood.
More horrible than any summing: the ruler in the egg.

Let's speak of things at the part when we first meet.
Each triumph must endure its morning after.
More enveloping than any atmosphere: two faces.

Let's speak of things that hold the moment together.
Are your faults trustworthy? Are you my wisdom?

One day the world will be as we thought we wanted it,
though we'll be carried in the mistral and haboob.
And we won't be ashamed our want had been so small.
Think of it now — how else could it be ours?

(That was the year you …)

That was the year you painted
a gate blue, a foreign year,
and the fishing boats in the village harbor
nodded
with some desire
at your thighs wrapped in a faded green sarong.

The gate was burred, the found brush stiff. You worked
the thickening color like heat
into a sore shoulder.

Beyond it stood the older man's cabana,
a thousand bound canes.
Remember
how you smeared yourself
with damp, black sand
for him, for yourself?

You burned and peeled
and feared
no mistakes among the bougainvillea.

You liked the effect
you had on people —
the gringa with ideas
like an invisible tub of wash balanced on her head.

Across the gorgeous cliffs nearby, goats followed you,
and panic was the drug that drowned
the drunk or macho
body surfers
at the dangerous beach below. On restaurant sands,
you met the sophomore girl you were
six months before

at *hora feliz*. Sometimes

she bought the shell necklaces and roach clips
you were learning how to make
after you had
everything
ripped off.
And you made her dicker,
if shy. You never begged
in the usual way.

The older man knew that, proud of his exile
from a war before your birth,
frightened of your age. He shared it
like his offered shoulder bearing
the ziggurat tattoo …
and the silver filigree of his smile.

Odor of wood smoke and shit and floral night falling.
When did those things become time
to move on?

Your acquisitive lives would not remain
abandoned.
And now you're glad
to make your way
like the blind, expatriate hippie
become a landlord,
toeing the wet edge along that shore —

past the orphanage
and the cafe of Delicate Carlos,
past geckos and wasps on night walls near light bulbs,

past the point
                  of your wisdom
and a gate still wet
                        to the touch.

(All the gossip ...)

All the gossip about your nearly nefarious son
who might not finally apply school to himself
          and turn out okay;
all the speculation and advice behind your back

about your sacrifice and yet unwillingness
to keep him to your curfews (what can she be thinking?);
          all the fretting
and resolve and fear for the fate young men choose,

reminds me of the watching on a bright, seared beach
where a fleshy, pale woman holds a baby in one arm;
          with her other hand,
she clutches a small parasol; she doesn't walk far

before the child she won't lower to the hot sand yet
grows too heavy. How to go on, then, and shield
          both from that light?
And, soon, how much shade, in turn, for each?

(Don't trust a man ...)

Don't trust a man who loves sea clouds
more dependably than his wife — ignore me, Tommy,

though Mars won't get this close to us again for 60,000 years.
Friends are furtive worms. They nudge the lie in life.

Fact: the zebrafish can grow back most of its heart.
Though why would it — or you — lose heart at all?

Fact: you're acting like a shit, it's said (and said often now),
because you've been ill, you're husbandless and sixty;

you don't show up, you leave others with the bill,
you expect a party in your honor and bedside worry

at your latest episode (this, after a few nights
dancing till dawn and perhaps just one more old-fashioned).

No one's had the gumption yet to pop you on the brow
and ask: what did you do with the wry pontificator

who charmed the beach weekends? Where's
the matchmaker of laughter and forethought?

Okay, a man can change ... Don't we hear *that*
and yet ignore it like another wrinkle at the ear ...

Maybe you *have* become wise, if you're freed
by carelessness, however calculated.

Fact: tear begs of tear, "Brother, where have you been?"
And who hasn't felt time as water bulging at the brim,

his needle on the surface, pointing nowhere special?

Does that qualify one for bathos? True, the cheating past

didn't kiss my in-flight magazine over Kansas. And comfort
sounds like a cancer survivor in the local shopper.

You're probably smart to punish the future now, given
who you've always been about to be, and duped by it.

(To ascend the mountain day ...)

To ascend the mountain day with white water at your shoulder,
with a berry-freighted gut and all bushes still drooping red.
To see the snake vanish into tart grass fit for teething,
to sit on a stone that does nothing to insist you move.
A walking stick, once a limb, rests against a spruce trunk.
A white butterfly flutters to show the bee it's not a flower.
No companion, this stream roiling against rock, this perpetual
composure.
No love in the frigid clarity of flow wearing down infinitesimally.
You rise, step through it, over it, figuring how. You note the path.
What is it behind you, pausing, that watches from the aspen eyes?
What do you taste, cupping the moment in your hand?
Around a bright nothing, gnats whirl. And your balance?
Lean forward and climb, the sun a wheel between your shoulders.
No peak awaits, no summing up, no wisdom in turning back.

(When you stretch out ...)

When you stretch out on a live oak limb,
        taking a pause from a hike to your conscience,
when you sense that tremor rising through the bark,

        here's your chance to understand politics.
Nearly everybody wants to make things right,
        but like you they're otherwise obligated,

and time, if it ever was theirs, isn't theirs anymore,
        for now, for the foreseeable, forever.
Lie back. Let that deep shiver rise through you.

        Is it an ancient quake from a hijacked state,
the bombing in the dust for justice, a check written?
        Or is it merely a heartbeat, perhaps your own?

Vernal or not, paths are most venal, dear niece.
        And that's not the same as Nature making us
hypocrites. We speak for ourselves, even as echoes.

The Dhawo

The Dhawo is coming to you friendly and able
With a goatee and a wrench and an admirable degree
You can't live long enough to exceed its plans to justify
It will redefine the way you do things most of all in private
The Dhawo has always been young and most promising most willing
most becoming
The Dhawo knows what is best for your town
There is no improvement without the Dhawo no loss for reminiscence
You may have wanted fame too but you must move over must be buried
now dear one

Don't pray to the Dhawo it thinks that's a tone for pitying yourself you
excuse
It halves the stone the cloud and has more surface
The lingo of computation the new the lingo of summation the new it
hears this
It will take every path from you and give them back in time for
pretending
The Dhawo is never lonely so it doesn't need your love
The Dhawo is ever wandering feeding on the human wish to figure out
It storms the city and casts down the silver drops the million flattering
mirrors useless to revelation
It wants to make your palm the shelf for this fall's product line

The Dhawo doesn't know it's the Dhawo it thinks it's hope a good
injection one of us
See its corpse-pile its rationale its artistic breakthrough its smooth cheek
Poor Dhawo never falls out of itself
Poor Dhawo speeds up
You can lick its creams you can vote for its opposition recycle seek
a real cave
The Dhawo with its myriad arms poor Dhawo hurts to have to do this
It jump cuts from evil it's coming ruddy and muscular

Tessitura

1.

Still joined,
these two don't look into their eyes
or away,

they neither whisper nor drowse.
The grand operas
they fancied loss might be,

those ecstatic arias,
are pitched
for more intriguing voices.

The places
other mouths found in them
never to hear

are elsewhere, if anywhere.
These two are rare
for this moment, improvising

the repose
no one couple keeps,
the textures

which sleep most often smoothes.
Days vanish
into diaries; and the avenue below,

trembling
with those going out for the night,
flatters them.

They are here. Who knows
their thoughts
though they conduct a tacit thing?

2.

Love has given me
More skin, more shadows.

More death at chance,
More memory and touch.

For the chores, a whetstone.
For the clouds, further gazes.

To the cozy wars,
Love has given me.

Love has taken me
From my gestures, my book,

From the barbed seed mother,
From the monopolist's pine.

Through each fatality, to a pebble.
Through immeasurable data.

Peeled yet wholly secret,
Love has taken me.

Love has broken me
with leaves, horizons.

Like bedsprings in a stream.
Like the mirror eaten away.

More give to bliss.
More terror in the waking.

Into room and its echo,
Love has broken me.

Poem

You with dried come on your thigh,
  that scar you've always faked for love —

you, betraying in your untoward sureness —

may time mash a wolf spider into your crotch;

roadside trash bags, brittle and split — know now
  what the wind will do with your guts,

you who tell the poor that waiting is a diamond:
  smell your alias;

aloneness aloneness — a vacant anthill in moonlight:
  lie on it on nine centuries,

promiser of sweet reunions, eventual justice,
  and don't look at me like that;

some only speak when they've finally died,
  their mirror crushed into fine, sharp powder;

they've met the hero of appearances;
  you who rip pleasure from pleasure, truth from truth,

the lamp rusts but the flame doesn't age;
  may your mind pit;

may all you've fingered nab you at the nape, inconsolable.

(The man who melts …)

The man who melts a plastic garbage bag
into a dagger, this inmate fearing other inmates,
has a point to make, a mark.
He understands a different courtesy
than we who read of his self-reliance
in a magazine designed to move.
Who merits the conviction in this artificer?
His innocence and ours persist beyond dispute.
To sneak it back to the daily cell,
its rumpled black edge like an ancient flint —
to know it's ready there —
secures the world and reforms the times.
Go through his pockets, you won't find it.
Frisk your soul, someone's relative as well,
and think of decency, of vengeance and empathy.
Think of the chances at lights out.

A Bicycle Called Forever

— China, 1986

In the compound dining hall, we foreigners
(friends through a common tongue) hush
as one recounts his Chinese student's tale:
her father, in the mad times,
holding pails of shit at arm's length —
a sentence to remind him of his crime
(a handshake he could not recall).
Our raptness, born of quieter childhoods,
barely shifts when he concludes
there was flirtation in her telling
and the diligence of one practicing a language.
In the silence before more rounds of rice,
we share, however slightly,
the edgy dumbness of the lucky —
for, after all, we cycle down these streets on those Forevers
sold only by permit to the privileged;
we've found discretion in our stacks of local currency
worthless elsewhere; and we're impressed
by bullet holes in cornices,
the Western clock with hands torn off —
the slide from civics to vendetta
no less blinding than our simple awe.
A cough comes through the window,
last night's soot in the woman
shoveling rough sand through wire mesh;
and further out, late for lunch, our compatriot
who always tells us later,
stops to watch a man's arms suddenly unfold
(right, dragon; left, clown) and children laugh.
Bicycle bells surround him:
Watch out! Sell it! Get on that thing and move!

A Contribution to the Time Capsule

There were the legs one pulled off certain moments,
baffled and compelled by the grasp.
And the hour dislocated suddenly like a shoulder
that must still lift the child.
If one wanted only blue, green was given.
If one lived for pine, one found oak.
Yet there was the rainbow in the rooster's black tail.
There was mind: a flock of swallows.
And thought: the shape of its flight.
To you in the future, forgive this our crudity.
Whatever our former tests, we were untested.
We needed hope, and our words
sometimes turned to cinders in our mouths.

(It's prideful, of course ...)

It's prideful, of course, but I admit I love poorly —
which is not the same as, in youth, confessing
I've been a lousy lover. Age makes us grateful for love,
so attention is welcome even by the suffering and betrayed;
even spouses will hope we might become what they think we were.
They don't want that so much as the poetry in our pockets now.

The spouses go to bed early, yes, at this time of marriage.
And, remaining, we're relieved and disturbed by not knowing
how to perform as we have for other years.
We might well perform again when shown how we undid.
There *are* things to say in this. But the things avoided
are not so much unsaid as wordless.

One sits alone and is not one. One does the last dishes
and wonders should the next page in the novel be turned?
Should the wine in the glass enter one? The triumph
is discovering that there's still pleasure and satisfaction,
though it's difficult without the unmockable look.
How far dare I go with this before I fall asleep and sober up?

How far does anybody go when they enter or receive?
No one knows when it's the beginning. Oh, the hands,
my hands, are assured in memory. My heart —
not much different from every protagonist.
I'm faithful to habit, hating its romance, and I'm breaking.
Love, I know you are, too, and just as frightened.
Yet there are no words because time is with us and against us.

(You with your face and I with mine ...)

You with your face and I with mine
neither ours but ours as much as anything
You here and I here both here and each a there
not ours but ours as much as anything
We have come this way in the shape of us now
And the instant of this stunning will vanish
will leave us to love and the order of touching
appearances as captive as we

You with your eternity and I with mine
neither ours but ours as much as anything
Who knows how to kiss the day into meaning
how to grasp their turn at the beautiful
We kiss we kiss oh so humanly kept
from revenge on the present unbelonging
We woo the instant of the stunning to return
not ours but ours as much as anything

(You're familiar with that sort ...)

You're familiar with that sort, who hugs harder as he doubts.
And with the State Highlights, given way like failed advertisements.
The integrity of monsters, too, is well-documented.
So tell me, Nick, how one forsakes our past for the current official lie.
Tell me how friendship endures a harvest of those shadows.

All have some right to their collapse, and to the little hooking epiphanies.
Most have the chance to look into the leaves before they join them.
Do you think the undeceived dead believe our fear is original?
Do you think they haven't waited to be finished off with our new meanings?
One can touch the doubled scar, Forgiveness. Though more than that is
needed.

Our age is a reckless feeding, a pleading through a window in the night.
Maybe it's a fairer time than most, as our possessions swear.
But how does one answer for the disarticulation as a joke?
I don't know you, nor you me. We knew, once. Before the drawn lightning.
Before you must have come to think we'd grown up to tremble like this.

(Do we try to appreciate ...)

Do we try to appreciate our vultures?
They float around our downtown office towers
like surrealist eyelashes. And we gaze upward:
        autumn in Tampa,

the seasonal return to these best perches,
most loyal thermals. Less focused on our business, then,
we might think of bankers, also circling
        the fortieth floor,

entranced by a respect for parsimony —
their carry-on for flights toward quick retirement.
Both know their numbers, they with the longer view
        toward beach developments ...

Harsh and unfair to compare buzzards to bankers.
The former love our town for what it is.
There are too many of them to electrocute,
        as pundits proposed.

A poet once praised the robins stopping here
for two or three ripe berry days. That was spring,
a different interest in the juicy, blue meat.
        Who reads it now?

Others want to live in towers, or around them.
Their livelihood burgeons in denial, in spoiling.
If they could own, they would, with a reckoning
        beyond possessives.

And others would bring all such purchase down,
just executing what they can for their Invisible.
Vultures wouldn't fall for it — at least not at first,
        then judiciously, quite.

Amorous Ode

1.

With faith
enough
          in consistent air,
or no will
to end
          serenity,
the flyer
anchored
          the kite by its string
to the trunk of a sabal palm.

A black diamond,
it floats
in the shoreline dusk,
          so tempting
to see it
          as our love:
a bargain between
starlight
and crossed ribs
          held aloft by thin skin.

Gone, perhaps,
to those glowing houses
built flush to the ground —

or those on stilts
          for the next hurricane —

did the flyer trust
our kind
          not to cut

the string so elegantly
binding creation?

We admired it
and against it
leaned
            our kiss.

2.

The mind's middle-of-the-night
filibuster.
            Have you heard it?
Some obstructionist
minority
            in what inner Congress,
it believes
it's right to delay
dreaming.

What does it hope
to weary us of?

What death does it prevent
us from knowing?

In rooms almost empty
            of ourselves, we've cried.
            Isn't that praying?

The rose has opened
on us
mussed by passion;

and, afterward,
pleasing,
you've laughed me out of you.

3.

Who are you
handing me
a washed plate
to dry?

Who am I,
answering
your thousand thrown voices?

You, spirit,
made me
stop
enumerating experience.
You leave
rooms lit
with their doors closed.

Are they then filled?

Who are you, throwing
yourself
heavily into my chairs,
my atmosphere?

Who am I,
wearing your colors?

Through flesh
I chased you

before I knew
            you existed.

4.

No?

Your brother
            from another time zone
runs along the surf —
            in his stride:

            your gawky gait,
            and the gait of the great blue heron
            just before it flies.

Rays bank in the green shallows,
brown kites,
brown diamonds.

You dare
            yourself
to shuffle in
            among their stingers,
            you of the leap.
Sandy clouds rise from your feet.
Whose courage?

Your forms surround me.
And not quite mistaken,
you call me
            by your brother's name.
            You call him by mine.

5.

Lucky,
I have no word
            for you.
This brings me, searching,
back to the page.

Back to you
who revises me
as I write you.

I've felt you suddenly
fall asleep
in my arms —
your weight
            in the awake world
then mine.

I hold it as I imagine
you would.

I will not fail
it
in any way
            I know.

6.

We postpone nothing
with our pleasure,
            that paper airplane
licked on the tip
            dipping
over spice sacks

in the oldest marketplaces.

    We see the mad men
    sleeping under the bridge.
    We see the battered wife
    murdered
    in newsprint.
    The purchased election.
    The censored massacre.
    The mud slides slithering
    down clear-cut hills.
    And the educated lies.
    And our lies.

We postpone
    nothing
with our pleasure.

We cast off
    futures.

    We dance, now, and only now.
    Dance, though our bones are bashful.
    Dance, among the stingers,
        and the hopes on stilts.

7.

The placid undulations of the bay
    explode
    the reflected moon

and recombine it —

yank it and squeeze it,

like some eternal clay,
in revenge, perhaps,
for its command of tides.

Over us,
the lit palm fronds
droop
like graying bangs,

and the heron
sometimes perches
on our chimney.

Years!

Yet your heat ripens
bananas into leopards,

your wit forgives
cruel mirrors,
and the wrinkled mind.

What revenge
can the years seek
unrecognized
in these eyes,
with no place in this world?

—for L.

(Last year's leaf …)

Last year's leaf like a stained glass window
with panes knocked out by a riot or temblor —
only its stem and veins, like leads, remain …
No nakedness we've known could be revealed
by its falling away. Black backs it best —
loam-hues: high contrast with its former skies
and ours. It haunts the palm, in life-lines there
long after it's been slipped into a book.
Those folds and leads outline the cupped flesh
of all our sacred wrecking. We profane
as we profess to hold ourselves for later.
Here is our beauty, discovered, hunted.
Inimitable touch, this leaf picks us.

Who's Long For Now?

See the star at evening, light more ancient than love? Hear the fruit rustle his fill in the bough? When I die,

some dead will die a little more. And I will die as you die, until we're done. Mother, lover, brother, foe,

to what do we owe allegiance till we're joined? I look to the side of my early wisdom, through the dark ringing that first halo. In a dream I try to recognize the grin of one who quotes to us our humiliation. How dare I wish to comprehend and to say, just once … despite this *me* so *me* no style can conceal it. To let the woods blow all over it, the burst pod shake the airy guts into the future —

enough perhaps. Who isn't younger when he enters into sleep? The beautiful get their beauty and the beauty of its loss. Even a wren takes its *there* when it lifts from the branch.

Distance joins things. A blue handkerchief in the ruins. Forgive it for belonging to Sue, who disappeared in that collapse. Now she's every age she'd been.

Would she have wept into it for one unlike her? Would those have been her tears? I didn't know her. She was herself — related to me by breath and the Beast springing from afar, nearby, to devour.

My home. *My* justice. *My* everlasting. That handkerchief dreamed, and dreams still. It can't be identified.

I've seen men dancing with imagined partners,

their arms around imagined waists, their hands in hands composed of the invisible; men this way grieving with their stricken friend drunk-desperate for his vanished life, her sway to common music … I've seen men unafraid to dance with nothing, with memory of all to come, coaxing up the comfortless and putting on the tune in a living room next door to History …

Cradling a notebook, what's your god-angle?

It occurs, nonetheless —

the sudden immersion of things in us brimming, brimming, unable to spill. The red fox bounding down the draw

glances back at you. *Why am I anyone?* you want to howl. *Or anyone me?* Behind you, the meadow tilts up toward dusk and the approaching years beneath the gauzy black scat, beneath the stubborn snow pocked and gritty in those same spring shadows. You wonder who hasn't stalked a path and muttered for himself. Who hasn't shied from shouting into such a vastness when he's had the chance. In those same surrounding woods near where the fox looks back once more and enters, you could mistake your childhood friend for your father bald and stooped and toeing toward his grave. You might even tell your friend of this and sit with them both in a silence not so much shared as suddenly caught on everything.

There are the revelations like transplanted marrow. Save your warm-up tears forever. The poem must now be useful, a knife mined from a fallen meteor. We're not leaving this place behind like any place we've been.

To look into the eye, say, of the one you have entered, to hold yourself there against the minute cloud white and shining at the center of the pupil … Don't try to speak as you hold its limbs down, smiling, yes, trying to smile, to show your meaning. Remember, if you can, the passengers on the ferry, who, rushing to witness a fight on the side deck,

capsized all …

Let our jokes be whispered. Let our kisses smart. Here is our information eating itself sweetly

as the black snout gouges through the vitals, as the boy from the terraced poor begs for the visitor's ballpoint pen while he shoves her boat from his village shore. The pale blue egg is falling toward your roof. The head of state becomes a headless statue.

Of the world's hostages who want to become its confidante (as if they could talk it into giving up its desperate plan) we might inquire: Do even the dullest hopes deserve a gentle chance? We can guess

which proverb lies closest to the nest. In the side of the plainest dwelling, beneath broken clapboard, a hive hums for the one who allows honey to gather, who takes it with the stings. *Self*, you might call it, but it won't answer to that. We're too lonely to be our own (and our loneliness too preciously human). The gift

is for the giver, the old encroachments for spring. Humiliation is pawned for vision, insight for loud silence. Can you, too, feel them darken with each evening fence?

In a teahouse in Chengdu, a man stuck a feathered wire delicately into a customer's ear and held to it a struck tuning fork. (It once seemed the sudden, steady-handed tone after you've thought someone, or something, to death. But no, not now, just a cleaning. Just.) Over speckled buttes near Santa Fe and the pools of withdrawn starlets, beside the roses eaten by Florida squirrels, around the ancient couple (she wearing his guitar, he bantering with a hubcap dealer) there appears a bewildering impasse. Again, no. The undulating red roof tiles: days of peace, the mind

thinking it's ready. *No* can bear more. *No* with the craze lines in its wisest smile. Poetry's all that's left of the soul when the soul's gone. What is it after the talk and silence, after the touch, beyond the continents uniting and dispersing, spurred by a minute star?

Madly a roach circles the lanai

until the cat comes to play. We're offered this like wine glasses crossed on restaurant tables, the blue jeans unzipped around a pregnant belly, smoke pouring from a grin as money passes through iron bars. We're presented *to* it

like the repetition in aristocratic wives after their husbands have been overthrown, roughening their hands with gravel to show the revolutionaries they're one of them, have always been working poor. It's palms up

versus feeling guilty about living well while people suffer. Artifice wins. And who doesn't hate it for not being what we'd wished? It replies:

You want some more poignant drooping of an orchid?

So there.

Admit the love broken by the six-thousandth *yes.* Make way for the blessing already rendered. Crime scenes are unsealed, refurbished and rented. Make way, if you can,

for something older, larger than oblivion. Hold a pine cone, its many barbed petals,

and try to feel each one swirled from the stem from the branch from the trunk

from the loam cool and wet around the cores below, beyond;

hold the viewpoints digging into the flesh now, the immigrant home and each green life unmoved to wander; hold the tongues from a seed,

for a seed, these cutting, mute tongues, the unknown impersonating
us myriad and singular;

we can't keep it away, can't let it fall away

though it has fallen around us, is falling still, so still, so still a der-
vishing on the copper waves of pine straw.

About the Author

Donald Morrill is the author of a previous collection of poetry, *At the Bottom of the Sky* (winner of the *Mid-List* First Series Award) and three books of nonfiction, *The Untouched Minutes* (winner of the *River Teeth* Literary Nonfiction Award), *Sounding for Cool* and *A Stranger's Neighborhood.* He has been a recipient of the *Missouri Review* Editors' Prize for Nonfiction and has been a Fulbright Lecturer in American Literature at the University of Lodz, Poland. He teaches at the University of Tampa and is poetry editor at *Tampa Review.*

The Florida Poetry Series

The Secret History of Water
Silvia Curbelo

Braid
Mia Leonin

nearly Florida
James Brock

The Rimbenders
Lola Haskins

Musical Chair
Rhonda J. Nelson

How Men Pray
Philip F. Deaver

Luckily
Kelle Groom